Thai Takeout Cookbook 2021

Thai Food Takeout

Recipes to Make at Home

Disclaimer and Terms of Use

Effort has been made to ensure that the information in this book is accurate and complete. However, the author and the publisher do not warrant the accuracy of the information, text, and graphics contained within the book due to the rapidly changing nature of science, research, known and unknown facts, and internet. The author and the publisher do not hold any responsibility for errors, omissions, or contrary interpretation of the subject matter herein. This book is presented solely for motivational and informational purposes.

The recipes provided in this book are for informational purposes only and are not intended to provide dietary advice. A medical practitioner should be consulted before making any changes in diet. Additionally, recipes' cooking times may require adjustment depending on age and quality of appliances. Readers are strongly urged to take all precautions to ensure ingredients are fully cooked in order to avoid the dangers of foodborne illnesses. The recipes and suggestions provided in this book are solely the opinion of the author. The author and publisher do not take any responsibility for any consequences that may result due to following the instructions provided in this book. The nutritional information for recipes contained in this book are provided for informational purposes only. This information is based on the specific brands, ingredients, and measurements used to make the recipe and therefore the nutritional information is an estimate, and in no way is intended to be a guarantee of the actual nutritional value of the recipe made in the reader's home. The author and the publisher will not be responsible for any damages resulting in your reliance on the nutritional information. The best method to obtain an accurate count of the nutritional value in the recipe is to calculate the information with your specific brands, ingredients, and measurements.

Contents

Introduction

Thai cuisine has a character all its own. It is easily distinguishable from Chinese and other Asian cuisines. Thai cooking balances sweet, sour, salty, bitter, and spicy in its own unique way. But, as with all takeout recipes, popular Thai takeout dishes as we know them may no longer be considered authentic by purists. Thai takeout dishes are mostly westernized (though delicious) versions of their originals.

This recipe book will help you prepare your favorite recipes, in your home. Most are easy to make without losing that takeout feel. Cooking at home may take some work, but it's always healthier and more fun.

History

Thai food is the result of the meeting of East and West. It is said to be basically Chinese but with many touches — ingredients and cooking methods — from neighboring Asian as well as faraway cultures from Europe that give it its own type of flavor. Chilies were said to have been introduced by Europeans, while curries were brought to them from India. The Arabs, Persians, Burmese, Laotians, and Khmers are also said to have influenced Thai cooking. The Thais innovated using their own resources, toning down the spiciness using their own herbs, and substituting ingredients such as ghee with coconut oil and cow's milk with coconut milk. The characteristics of Thai food also vary depending on the region of origin. The northern regions, for example, are largely Chinese-influenced; while the southern regions are more heavily Malay -influenced. Thai food as we know it in the West is said to be reminiscent of the ancient royal cuisine of central Thailand or of the former Ayutthaya Kingdom. The many cultures that have contributed to the colorful and exciting flavors of Thailand are still certainly uniquely Thai. Thailand was never colonized, and was therefore able to maintain its own identity and its own cuisine. When the monarchy was overthrown in the 1940s, Thailand's first Prime Minister, Phibun, initiated a drive to further establish a strong cultural identity. The selling and consumption of foreign dishes was discouraged. Chinese street food was banned and a call was made to develop a dish that they could call their own. This brought about the invention of *Pad Thai (or Phat Thai)*, their national dish. Today, Thai restaurants are rated based on how well they make their Pad Thai.

Asian takeout in the Unites States began mainly with Chinese immigrants in the 1900s, but Thai takeouts only began to spring up much later. There may have been a very small number of Thai restaurants that were established from the late 50s to late 60s, but takeouts seem to have begun to mushroom in the 70s. Thai takeout in the West is seen by traditionalists as heavily westernized. Thai restaurants in the West are also restricted, perhaps, by the taste buds of the population as well as the availability of ingredients. Where authentic Thai cuisine is characterized by bold flavors, westernized Thai is bland in comparison. Westernized Thai dishes contain more and bigger-sized portions of meat and fewer portions of herbs. Dried shrimp, a mainstay in true Thai cooking, is sometimes absent in the West. Perhaps it is perceived as too funky for the western palate. In spite of this, many are becoming more adventurous and appreciative of the authentic flavors. Meanwhile, with the heavy influx of tourists from the West to Thailand, Thai chefs are now coming up with many more western-inspired and fusion dishes.

Ingredients in Thai Cuisine

Thailand has added its own ingredients to place its stamp on dishes that were introduced to them by foreigners such as the Chinese and Indians. You will usually find the following things in their dishes.

Black Pepper

Black peppercorns are used in many dishes and were the original source of heat in Thai recipes. Chilies were only introduced in the 16th century.

Chili Oil

Called *nam phrik phow,* this deep red oil is almost ever-present in Thai dishes and is more convenient to use than fresh chilies. It can be stored in the refrigerator, ready whenever it is needed.

Chilies

For stir-fries and sauces, Thai or Bird chilies are used. For curries, cayenne chilies are the most common choice. Dried chilies are also used to make curry paste or for stir-fries and soups. Chilies can cause pepper burn and irritate the skin, so use rubber gloves when handling them, and be careful not to get them into your eyes. Avoid inhaling their powder or their vapors when cooking, as this can irritate the respiratory tract.

Cilantro (*Pak Chee*)

This is the ubiquitous garnish in Thai cooking, which uses the leaves, stems, and roots of the plant. It is an aromatic herb that has a somewhat citrusy flavor. Some perceive its flavor as "soapy." It is usually used raw, as a garnish, as heat dissipates its flavor. Thais also value this herb for its medicinal properties. It is said to be good for digestion and removal of toxins from the body. It is also called *Chinese parsley* or *coriander,* though we will use the term coriander to refer to the seed of the plant.

Coconut Milk

Dairy may not be as popular and coconut milk is used instead. Canned coconut milk may also be used.

Curry Paste

This is an essential ingredient in Thai curries that gives them a distinct flavor. There is red curry paste, green curry paste, yellow curry paste, *Panang* curry paste, and *Massaman* curry paste. Each is composed of a unique combination of herbs and spices to give characteristic flavor. These can also be purchased ready-made at Asian stores.

Dried Shrimp

Kung haeng is used to add an umami element to Thai dishes. It is used to make chili and curry pastes. It is also an ingredient in Pad Thai as well as Thai salads.

Fish Sauce

Called *nam pla,* it made from fish (usually anchovies) fermented in brine. Most Thai dishes make more use of fish sauce rather than soy sauce to add saltiness and flavor. Vietnamese and Filipino versions are also available but vary in flavor and level of saltiness.

Galangal

This looks similar to ginger but is lighter in color with tinges of pink. It gives a distinct flavor, and fresh is best.. If you must use dried galangal, soak it first until it softens. Use 2 parts powdered to every 1 part fresh required in the recipe.

Herbs

Fresh herbs such as cilantro, mint, Thai basil, and Vietnamese coriander are ever-present in a variety of Thai dishes.

Lemongrass
Also called *takraii,* it gives a lemony flavor plus a hint of ginger. It may also be used dried or in powder and paste. When used fresh to make a paste, grinding or bruising using a mortar and pestle is said to better release its flavor.

Lime
Limes are used to achieve zest and sourness in Thai dishes. Lime is used in soups and curries to add tartness and aroma. It also has a tenderizing effect on meat.

Noodles
Thais use many different kinds of noodles. Here are just a few:

Bean Noodles (Wun Sen)
Bean noodles or mung bean noodles, are also called transparent noodles, glass noodles, cellophane noodles, or thread noodles. There are different ways of cooking and preparing these noodles, depending on the recipe. They become pliable when soaked in hot water, and translucent when cooked.

Wide Rice Noodles (Sen Han)
Large rice noodles often used in stir-fries. Commonly used for Drunken Noodles (*Pad Kee Mow*) and Stir-Fried Soy Sauce Noodles (*Pad See Ew).*

Medium Rice Noodles/Rice Sticks (Sen Lek)
The noodles used to make Pad Thai. They are about the same size and appearance as linguine.

Rice Sticks/Thin Rice Noodles (Sen Yai)
The thinnest, flat rice noodles that are used in soups and stir fries.

Rice Vermicelli (Sen Mee)
These are the thinnest round type of rice noodles and may be mistaken for bean noodles. They also need to be soaked in water before adding to dishes, and are white in color when cooked.

Palm Sugar

A sweetening ingredient made from the sap of the palmyra palm. If you buy it in tubs, check for softness by flexing the tubs. If it's too hard, warm it in the microwave to soften it. You may pound or grate it into a powder or soak it in water to soften it into syrup. It may also be bought in paste form, which is more convenient to use. Many recipes call for ordinary refined cane sugar, but palm sugar is said to be more flavorful. Coconut sugar and muscovado sugar are similar in flavor and are suitable substitutes.

Pandan Leaves

Bai teoy hom, as it is called, lends aroma and flavor to Thai dishes. Meats and fish are sometimes wrapped in pandan leaves. It can be used in savory and sweet dishes and even to flavor drinks. If you can't find the leaves, you can use pandan extract.

Plum Sauce

A sweet, sour, and spicy sauce used as a dip or flavorful sauce for dishes.

Rice

Sticky rice and jasmine rice are commonly used to partner meat and vegetable dishes. It is also used to make snacks and desserts. Sticky rice is more often eaten in the northern region of Thailand while jasmine rice is more common in the south.

Rhizome (*Krachai* or *Gkrachai*)

Ginger and galangal are also rhizomes, but this is thinner and smaller and is also called lesser ginger, fingerroot or Chinese ginger. It is not a very well-known ingredient in the West but, in authentic Thai cuisine, it is used in salads, stir-fries and in Jungle Curry. Its flavor is described as mildly medicinal and it is said to be good for digestion. You may be able to buy this frozen or pickled in brine.

Shallots and Garlic

These are chopped or minced and usually sautéed. They're used in many dishes.

Shrimp Paste (*Kapi*)

This an essential ingredient in dips, sauces, and curry pastes, made from ground shrimp fermented in salt. It is used in making curry pastes and dipping sauces. It has a foul smell and some mistakenly think it is rotten or inedible.

Sriracha Sauce

A popular condiment made from chilies, vinegar, garlic, and sugar. The Rooster brand, which is most popular in the US, was made by a Vietnamese immigrant. It is named after a town (Si Racha) in Thailand, where the sauce originated.

Sweet Chili Sauce

Nam chim kai is a popular condiment for many Thai recipes, especially appetizers. It is made of chilies in vinegar and garlic.

Tamarind

Mahahm is used to give food a sour note. The pods or the pulp may be used, although tamarind blocks or paste can also be bought and are convenient to use. Possible substitutes are vinegar, lime juice, HP sauce, or dates crushed in lemon.

Thai Basil

A variety of sweet basil. The taste of Thai basil or *horapha* is said to be a mixture of anise and licorice. This basil has a higher heat resistance than sweet basil, although sweet basil can be substituted in recipes. This is used in Drunken Noodles (*Pad Kee Mow*) and curries. Most Thais prefer Holy Basil (*kaphrao*), which lends a peppery, clove-like flavor.

Thai Pepper Powder

Known as *prik Thai*, it is mainly composed of white pepper with a bit of coriander and garlic. Is used to achieve an *umami* taste.

Vinegar

Rice vinegar is commonly used to add sourness or as an ingredient for dipping sauces and salad dressings. White distilled vinegar or apple cider vinegar may also be used although the resulting flavor will differ a bit.

Common Tools and Equipment

Thai cooking does not require highly-specialized equipment. It is possible to prepare their dishes with what is available in any conventional kitchen. Here are some tools that are commonly found in a Thai kitchen.

Chopping Block

Wooden chopping blocks are used for chopping meat and fish.

Cleaver
Usually just this one large knife is sufficient for making a variety of cuts and slices for meats and vegetables. The flat side can be used for crushing or smashing garlic or pieces of ginger.

Coconut Grater
This used to be indispensable for preparing dishes requiring coconut milk, but canned coconut milk has made this unnecessary. However, those who prefer freshly-prepared coconut milk still have this in their kitchen. Freshly grated or frozen shredded coconut can also be purchased.

Coconut Shell Spoon
This is the traditional ladle for cooking. But any modern ladle will do.

Curry Pot
A traditional clay pot with large handles, exclusively for making curry dishes. A heavy-bottomed cooking pot can be used instead.

Food Processor
This will be useful in preparing curry pastes and sauces. Using a mortar and pestle is more tiresome and time consuming but, if you do, the resulting flavor is said to be superior.

Glutinous Rice Basket
A clever invention for cooking and keeping glutinous rice. It is a bamboo basket which ensures that the rice achieves the right stickiness and fluffiness. It also prevents the sticky rice from spoiling easily, but it may be impractical for the modern cook. A splatter guard, fine-meshed metal sieve, or colander may be used instead.

Mortar and Pestle
Traditionally made of stone and used to bruise lemongrass leaves and herbs and to crush garlic. Also used to prepare curry pastes.

Skewer
Made of bamboo and used for grilling.

Spatula or turner
This are valuable especially for stir-fries.

Steamer

This was traditionally used to cook sticky rice and is ever-present in a Thai kitchen. The rice cooker is the modern replacement.

Strainer

Useful for straining liquid or oil from other ingredients such as noodles or fried meats.

Wok

The quintessential Asian cooking pan. Useful for stir-frying, deep-frying and a host of other cooking methods. Any ordinary frying pan can be used in place of a wok.

Cooking Methods

Thai cooking normally does not require any complicated method of cooking. Thai dishes are usually simple to prepare and sparing in the use of oil.

Stir-Frying

A quick, low-fat and nutrient-preserving method of cooking, in which ingredients are cooked in an ultra-hot wok with minimal oil and frequent stirring. The result is a hot, fresh dish of crisp and tasty ingredients. The key to stir-frying is to start with a very hot wok before adding oil. Prepare all the ingredients in advance and have them ready before stir-frying. Toss seafood quickly to seal in juices.

Steaming

Steaming seals in flavor, nutrients, and freshness. Place a heat-proof dish over boiling water and cover it with a tight-fitting lid to keep the steam in.

Stewing

This method involves slow cooking to soften meats and to seal in flavor. Ingredients are cut up into similar sizes and covered with water, and then simmered. The liquid may be served with the dish or reduced to make gravy.

Deep frying

This is usually done in a wok filled about half-way with oil. The oil must be heated to 350°F before adding ingredients to be fried. Keep heat-proof tongs, a slotted spoon, or a strainer ready to fish the fried food out of the hot oil. It is best to drain the deep-fried food on paper towels to keep it crisp.

Grilling

Food such as meat and fish are sometimes cooked over coals or flame. Sometimes the food is wrapped in *pandan* or banana leaves to impart flavor and reduce charring. Modern cooks now use aluminum foil. Heat must be well-regulated to ensure even cooking.

Now that you've got your ingredients and utensils ready, it's time to start cooking!

Appetizers

Classic Spring Roll (Poh Pia Tod)

Serves: 8-16
Preparation Time: 10 minutes plus 20 minutes soaking time
Cooking Time: 15-20 minutes

Ingredients
<u>Sweet chili sauce</u>
1 cup water, divided
4 teaspoons cornstarch
2 teaspoons fresh ginger, minced
1 teaspoon garlic, minced
4-6 pieces Thai chili, minced
1 cup rice vinegar
½ cup sugar
2 teaspoons ketchup

Sweet plum sauce
1 Japanese salted pickled plum
5 tablespoons sugar
1 tablespoon rice vinegar
2-3 tablespoons water

Spring rolls
4 dried shiitake mushrooms
3 ounces bean thread noodles
1 tablespoon vegetable oil
3 cloves garlic, minced
5 medium to large prawns, cleaned, peeled and minced (or about 3-4 ounces ground pork or beef)
½ cup carrot, peeled and shredded
2 tablespoons soy sauce, preferably light
1 teaspoon sugar
½ teaspoon Thai pepper powder
1 cup fresh bean sprouts
2 tablespoons chopped spring onion
2 tablespoons chopped cilantro
16 fresh spring roll wrappers

Flour paste
2 tablespoons flour or cornstarch
1 tablespoon water

Directions
Underline For sweet chili sauce

1. In a cup or small bowl, mix 1 tablespoon of the water with the cornstarch. Set it aside.
2. Pound the ginger, garlic, and chili in a mortar and pestle to make a paste. Note: use rubber gloves when handling chili peppers to avoid pepper burns.
3. In a saucepan, pour the vinegar, remaining water, sugar, and ketchup. Bring it to a boil.
4. Reduce heat and simmer, stirring occasionally, for 5 minutes.
5. Stir the water and cornstarch mixture again and whisk it into the

sauce. Stir until you notice some thickening.

6. Remove from the

heat. <u>For sweet plum sauce</u>

7. Place the ingredients in a small pot or saucepan and mash them together.
8. Bring them to a boil and continue boiling until they form a syrup.

<u>For spring rolls</u>

9. Soak the shiitake mushrooms in hot water for 10-20 minutes. Drain and squeeze out the excess water. Slice thinly, and set them aside.
10. Soak the noodles in water for 15 minutes. Drain and cut into 1-inch strands. Set aside.
11. In a small bowl, combine the flour paste ingredients and set it aside.
12. Heat the oil in a wok, and sauté the garlic until fragrant.
13. Stir in the minced shrimp, shiitake, noodles, and carrot.
14. Stir in the soy sauce, sugar, and pepper powder. Stir fry for 3-5 minutes.
15. Add the bean sprouts, spring onion, and cilantro. Mix to heat through, and remove to a bowl and allow the mixture to cool down.
16. Place one wrapper at a time on a clean surface or tray, in a diamond shape.
17. Add about 2 tablespoons of filling close to the tip of the diamond at the bottom or closest to you. Do not put too much filling or else the wrapper will break while frying.
18. Fold the bottom tip of the wrapper over the filling. Roll tightly once.
19. Fold the left and right corners inward, and continue rolling up to the top corner.
20. Moisten the top corner with the flour paste to seal the roll.
21. Repeat this process until all filling or wrappers are used up.
22. Fry the spring rolls until they are golden brown, in about one inch of vegetable oil. For more efficient heating and to get crisp rolls,

fry in batches, and do not overcrowd the rolls in the oil.

23. Use a spider strainer or tongs to lift rolls out of the oil, and place them in a dish lined with paper towels.

24. Serve hot with sweet-sour plum sauce or sweet chili sauce.

Sesame Fried Tofu

Serves: 4
Preparation Time: 5-10 minutes plus 20 minutes pressing time
Cooking Time: 15-25 minutes

Ingredients

12 ounces extra firm tofu
1 egg, lightly beaten
¼ cup cornstarch
¼ cup peanut or vegetable oil
1-2 tablespoons sesame seeds, lightly toasted

For sauce

1 garlic clove, minced
½ cup sugar
2 tablespoons cornstarch
¾ cup water
⅛ cup rice vinegar
2 tablespoons soy sauce
2 tablespoons sesame oil

1 teaspoon chili paste

Peanut dipping sauce
½ cup cilantro, chopped
1 teaspoon chili pepper, ground to a paste
2 tablespoons peanuts, toasted and crushed
1 pinch salt
2 tablespoons sugar
2 tablespoons vinegar

Directions

1. Place the tofu in a shallow baking pan lined with a tea towel. Top with another towel followed by another baking pan. Add something heavy (like a can of soup) to press down for 20 minutes, to squeeze out the liquid. Drain the tofu, and wipe it dry, then cut it into 2-inch squares, half an inch thick, cut in halves.
2. Dip the cubes in egg and then toss in cornstarch to coat. Shake to remove any excess cornstarch. Arrange the pieces on a tray or plate, and set aside.
3. In a small saucepan, mix together the ingredients for the sauce. Boil for 5 minutes, until thickened.
4. Meanwhile, heat the oil in a wok. Fry the tofu for 3-5 minutes, or until golden brown on the bottom. Flip over gently to cook other side. When the cubes are golden brown on both sides, remove them to drain on paper towels.
5. Remove the oil from wok, leaving about a tablespoon. Return the fried tofu cubes to the wok and pour in the thickened sauce. Stir gently to coat the tofu and sprinkle it with sesame seeds. Serve with dipping sauce.
6. To make the dipping sauce, combine the sugar, chili paste, salt, and vinegar in a microwavable bowl and heat until the sugar is dissolved (about 1 minute). Stir well and sprinkle with peanuts and cilantro.

Fresh Summer Rolls with Tamarind Sauce

Serves: 40-60 (as snack or side dish)
Preparation Time: 40 minutes
Cooking Time: 2-5 minutes

Ingredients
1 package rice wrappers small, round

Filling
2 tablespoons soy sauce
1 tablespoon rice vinegar
1 tablespoon fish sauce
1 teaspoon brown, palm sugar or muscovado
1 cup thin vermicelli rice noodles, cooked and rinsed in cold water, drained
½ cup cooked shrimp, finely chopped
½ cup fried tofu, julienned
½ cup roasted chicken, shredded
1 cup lettuce, julienned
½ cup cucumber, julienned

½ cup fresh Thai basil, roughly chopped
½ cup fresh coriander, roughly chopped
¼ cup carrot, shredded or julienned 3-4
spring onions, finely chopped

Tamarind dipping sauce
½ cup water
½ teaspoon tamarind paste
2 teaspoons sugar
1 tablespoon soy sauce
1 tablespoon fish sauce
1 teaspoon arrowroot or cornstarch powder, dissolved in 3
tablespoons water 1 clove garlic, minced
1 green or red chili, finely sliced

Directions

1. First, prepare the dipping sauce. Combine all the ingredients together in a saucepan. Bring to a near-boil and reduce heat. Continue cooking, stirring constantly, until the sauce thickens. Adjust the taste as needed. Remove from the heat and set it aside.
2. Set aside rice wrapper.
3. In a small bowl, whisk together the soy sauce, vinegar, fish sauce, and sugar. Set this mixture aside as well.
4. In a large bowl, combine all the filling ingredients. Pour in the soy sauce mixture and toss to coat.
5. Take a rice wrapper and submerge it in hot water (it should be tolerable to the touch). The wrapper should be of the right softness in 30 seconds.
6. Place the wrapper on a clean, flat surface and another wrapper from the package into the hot water.
7. Place a heaping tablespoon of filling about half an inch from the bottom of the wrapper. Spread out the filling to form a small rectangular shape.
8. Fold the bottom flap of the wrapper over the filling and tuck in the sides. Keep the roll tight as you roll from the bottom upwards. Moisten the top flap with a little water to seal.
9. Arrange the rolls, sealed side down, on a platter. You may slice the

rolls diagonally in half to reveal the colorful filling.
10. Serve with prepared tamarind sauce.

Thai Beef Jerky

Serves: 2-3

Preparation Time: 10 minutes plus 1-12 hours marinating time, 3-4 hours drying time
Cooking Time: 3-5 minutes

Ingredients

1 pound beef, cut into 3-inch by ½-inch pieces
2 cloves garlic, finely chopped
5 cilantro roots, crushed, or 2 teaspoons ground coriander
1 teaspoon pepper powder
3 tablespoons white sesame seeds
2 teaspoons sugar or honey
1 tablespoon fish sauce
2 tablespoons oyster sauce
1 tablespoon beef bouillon powder (optional)

Directions

1. Combine all the ingredients in a bowl. Using your hands, massage the seasonings into the beef thoroughly. Cover, and let it marinate for 1 hour to overnight (refrigerated).
2. Lay the beef strips on a rack and leave it in the sun for 3-4 hours, turning the beef occasionally.
3. If you want to use an oven, heat to 160°F and dry the beef in the oven for about 3 hours. When it's ready, the beef can be bent to break. If the beef is too dry, it will snap.
4. To fry, heat 2-3 tablespoons of oil in a wok and fry the beef strips until slightly caramelized.
5. Drain over paper towels.
6. Transfer to serving dish and serve with cucumber or tomato, chili or Sriracha sauce, and sticky rice.

Curry Puff

Serves: 12-25
Preparation Time: 20-30 minutes
Cooking Time: 25-30 minutes

Ingredients

Cucumber relish

1 cup rice vinegar

6 tablespoons sugar

1-3 teaspoons chili paste

2 tablespoons cucumber, peeled and finely chopped

1 tablespoon fresh cilantro, finely chopped

For pastry dough

3 cups all-purpose flour, divided

6 tablespoons vegetable oil, plus more for frying

½ cup cold

water For filling

2 tablespoons vegetable oil

1 small onion, minced

1 teaspoon Thai pepper powder

1 tablespoon butter (optional)

1 ½ cups chicken fillet, cut into quarter- or half-inch cubes (For a vegetable curry puff, omit the chicken and add 1 cup each of cubed carrots and green peas.)

1 ½ tablespoons curry powder

½ teaspoon cumin powder

2 teaspoons salt

1 tablespoon sugar

1 medium potato, peeled, cooked and cut into cubes

1 teaspoon ground white pepper

Directions

For cucumber relish

1. Whisk together the vinegar, sugar, and chili paste. Add the cucumber and coriander. Cover and keep in the refrigerator until ready to use.

For filling

2. Heat a wok over medium heat and add oil.
3. Add the onion, Thai pepper powder, and butter (optional). Sauté until the onion is translucent.
4. Add the chicken. Stir and cook until the chicken is almost done, about 8-10 minutes.
5. Add the seasonings, except the white pepper, and mix well.
6. Add the potatoes and continue cooking until they absorb most of the moisture.
7. Adjust the taste as needed. Ideally, the filling should be dry to prevent the dough from becoming soggy or bursting. It should also be a little salty, as the pastry will balance it out.
8. Turn off the heat and stir in white pepper powder. Set it aside and allow it to cool.

For pastry dough

9. Separate 1 cup of the all-purpose flour to another bowl. You will have 2 bowls of flour, one bowl with 1 cup and another with 2 cups.
10. Add a tablespoon each of oil into each bowl of flour. (As you continue, always add the same amount of oil to each bowl.)
11. Using your hand, mix the oil and flour in the bowl that has 1 cup of flour. Add another tablespoon of oil to each bowl and continue mixing with your hand. You will mix the contents of the second bowl (containing 2 cups flour) later.
12. Add a third tablespoon of oil to each bowl. The flour should start to adhere by now in the first bowl. This is the "oil dough." Set it aside.
13. To the second bowl, add the cold water and mix it together with one hand to make a smooth, slightly sticky dough. You may add a little more water if needed. Divide this dough into 5 roughly uniform pieces. Shape these into balls and flatten them using your palm and fingers to form discs. This is the "water dough."
14. Go back to the first bowl, or oil dough, and separate this into 5 pieces as well. These pieces are smaller than the ones in the previous bowl.
15. Take one of the smaller pieces of oil dough and place it in the center of one of the discs of water dough. Fold the sides of the disc over the small dough ball and pinch the edges to seal. Gently and lightly shape this dough "dumpling" into a ball but do not knead. Do the same for the rest of the dough.
16. Using a rolling pin, roll out a ball of dough to about ¼-inch thickness. Lift the lower end and roll up the dough like a scroll. Position the "scroll" vertically on the table surface and flatten again with a rolling pin. Again, roll to make a scroll. This scroll should be cylindrical in shape. Cut this cylinder into 5 equal pieces using a knife or dough cutter. You will have 5 small discs and you will see the layers of water and oil dough that form the disc.
17. Roll out one of this discs with a rolling pin into a thin circle, about a sixteenth to an eighth-inch thick.
18. Place about 1 ½ teaspoons to 1 tablespoon of filling (not too much or the pastry will break) close to the center of the dough and fold it over to form a semi-circle, with the filling inside. Flute or crimp

the edges by gently rolling the edge with your thumb and forefinger.

19. Heat oil for frying to 350°F (the dough will break apart if the oil is not the right temperature) and deep-fry until golden brown.

20. Drain over paper towels. Serve with cucumber sauce.

Crispy Chicken Wings

Serves: 6

Preparation Time: 20 minutes plus 6 hours marinating time and 20 minutes air-drying
Cooking Time: 25 minutes

Ingredients

4 pounds chicken wings

For tamarind dipping sauce

½ cup water
½ teaspoon tamarind paste
2 teaspoons sugar
1 tablespoon soy sauce
1 tablespoon fish sauce
1 teaspoon arrowroot or cornstarch powder, dissolved in 3 tablespoons water 1 clove garlic, minced
1 green or red chili, finely sliced

For marinade

6 large cloves of garlic, peeled
2 teaspoons whole coriander seeds
1 tablespoon whole white peppercorns
2 tablespoons cilantro roots or stems, finely chopped
3 tablespoons oyster sauce
2 teaspoons salt
1 teaspoon sugar

For batter
1 ½ cups rice flour
1 teaspoon salt
1 teaspoon chicken bouillon powder or granules
1 cup of water plus 2 teaspoons baking soda

For dry coating
2 cups of rice flour

Directions

1. First, prepare the dipping sauce. Combine all ingredients together in a saucepan. Bring it to a near-boil and reduce the heat. Continue cooking and stirring, until the sauce thickens. Adjust the taste as needed. Remove it from the heat and set aside.
2. Dry the chicken with paper towels and place it in a large bowl.
3. Make a paste by pounding the first four marinade ingredients in a mortar and pestle or food processor.
4. Add the paste and other marinade ingredients to the chicken, and rub it into the chicken with your hands.
5. Cover and let it marinade in refrigerator for 6 hours or overnight.
6. Whisk together the batter ingredients.
7. Coat the marinated chicken (do not drain or wipe off marinade) with the thin batter.
8. Follow this immediately with a coat of rice flour. Shake off some excess flour, and arrange the coated chicken on a tray or cookie sheet.
9. Let it air-dry for 15-20 minutes.
10. Heat up oil in a wok or fryer to 350°F.
11. Fry the chicken until the inside is thoroughly cooked and the

outside is golden brown.
12. Remove from the oil and drain it on a cooling rack over paper towels.
13. Serve with tamarind dipping sauce.

Thai Fish Cake

Serves: 10-15
Preparation Time: 20 minutes
Cooking Time: 10 minutes

Ingredients

<u>Cucumber Relish</u>
¾ cup Thai sweet chili sauce
½ cup cucumber, thinly sliced
2 tablespoons dry-roasted peanuts, finely chopped
2 tablespoon cilantro leaves, coarsely chopped
3 tablespoon shallots, thinly sliced

2 large egg whites
1 (4-ounce) can red curry paste
¼ cup sugar
4 tablespoons fish sauce
1 tablespoon paprika (optional)
1 ½ pounds fish paste (store-bought)

4 tablespoons chiffonade of kaffir lime leaves

1 cup Chinese long beans, finely chopped

½ cup chiffonade of basil leaves

Vegetable oil, for deep-frying

Directions

1. First, prepare the cucumber relish. Mix the ingredients for the relish together, cover, and refrigerate.
2. Meanwhile, mix together the egg whites, red curry paste, sugar, fish sauce and paprika, if using. Add the fish paste and mix to make a thick paste. Use your hands to mix, or use the paddle attachment of a stand mixer. Mix for about 5 minutes.
3. When the paste is mixed well and feels very sticky, fold in the kaffir lime leaves, long beans, and chiffonade of basil leaves.
4. Cover with plastic wrap and refrigerate for 30 minutes.
5. Heat a wok over medium heat and fill it with oil, about 2 inches deep. The temperature of the oil should be 350°F.
6. Prepare a small bowl of water to wet your hands so that the fish paste won't stick.
7. After wetting your hands, scoop out a handful of the fish paste mixture. Make a ball and flatten it to make about a 2-inch diameter patty.
8. Fry the fish patties until golden brown (about 30 seconds). Flip over to cook the other side. The patty should be cooked after about 1 minute of frying. The patties are done when they resist a bit or bounce when tapped while frying.
9. Remove the cooked fish cakes and drain on paper towels.
10. Serve with cucumber relish. May also be eaten with rice.

Crispy Fried Calamari

Serves: 4-6
Preparation Time: 10 minutes
Cooking Time: 10 minutes

Ingredients

1 pound squid tubes, cut into ½-inch rings (or use pre-cut rings)

2 cups semolina flour, divided

1 tablespoon teaspoon salt

1 tablespoon sugar

1-2 teaspoons dried crushed chilies or cayenne powder

1 teaspoon garlic powder

⅛ teaspoon 5-spice powder (optional)

⅛ teaspoon ground white pepper (optional)

2 eggs, lightly beaten

Vegetable oil for frying

Lettuce or fresh coriander leaves for serving

Lime wedges, for serving (optional)

Directions

1. Dry the squid rings with a towel.
2. Prepare 3 bowls. In the first bowl, place 1 cup of flour. The second bowl should contain the beaten eggs. In the third bowl, combine the remaining flour, salt, sugar, and spices. This is the coating mixture.
3. Prepare a tray for coated rings.
4. Take a ring and coat it with plain flour, gently shaking to remove any excess.
5. Next, dip it into the egg, then into the coating mixture.
6. Lay it on the tray. Do not let coated rings touch or else they will stick.
7. Repeat until all the rings are coated.
8. Pour oil into a wok or frying pan to 1-inch deep. Heat over medium-high, to 350°F. When the oil begins to shimmer, you can test it by placing a ring into the oil, it should begin to sizzle and cook.
9. Fry the rings in batches to avoid overcrowding and to maintain the right frying temperature, for about 1 ½ minutes on each side. You can use a skewer to flip the rings.
10. If the oil is too hot, it will splatter, so reduce the heat if necessary.
11. Fried rings should be light golden brown. Do not overcook or else the squid will turn rubbery.
12. Drain the cooked rings on paper towels.
13. Serve immediately with Thai sweet chili sauce.

Andaman Shrimp Cake

Serves: 4-6
Preparation Time: 10 minutes
Cooking Time: 20 minutes

Ingredients

7 ounces pork belly, cubed
5-6 cloves garlic, minced
1 teaspoon ground white pepper
1 cilantro root
1 pound shrimp meat
2 eggs
4 teaspoons sugar
2 tablespoons light soy sauce
⅓ cup all-purpose flour
2 cups Panko bread crumbs
Oil for frying

Directions

1. Combine the pork belly, garlic, pepper, and cilantro root in a food processor and grind to a coarse consistency.
2. Add 1/3 of the shrimp, eggs, sugar, soy sauce and flour into the food processor and continue grinding to a coarse but evenly-distributed mixture.
3. Add the rest of the shrimp and just pulse the food processor a few times.
4. To test, take a spoonful and microwave for 15 seconds. Make any needed adjustments with saltiness, sweetness, or spiciness accordingly. Add water if it's too dry.
5. Take 2 tablespoons of the shrimp mixture and flatten it into a patty using your hands, and coat with Panko bread crumbs.
6. Fry in 1-inch deep oil at 300°F, turning over now and then.
7. You must regulate the temperature so that patty is evenly cooked. The cake is done when it is golden brown outside and also well done inside.
8. Drain on paper towels.
9. Serve with sweet plum sauce or sweet chili sauce.

Crab Rangoon

Serves: 8-10
Preparation Time: 10 minutes
Cooking Time: 2 minutes

Ingredients

1 (6-ounce) can crabmeat
6 ounces cream cheese, softened to room temperature
3 cloves garlic, minced
1 dash Worcestershire sauce
½ teaspoon salt
1 dash white pepper
Wonton skins
1 beaten egg, for sealing
Oil, for frying

Directions

1. Combine the first 6 ingredients (through white pepper), mixing well.

2. Prepare the wontons and place a wrapper on a clean surface.
3. Spoon out about ½ teaspoon of filling for each wonton. Place in the middle of a wonton and pinch the opposite corners together.
4. Carefully squeeze out any air (this is very important, or else the filling make a mini-explosion when frying) and then seal the edges with the beaten eggs.
5. Deep-fry until golden brown, and drain on paper towels.
6. Serve with sweet chili sauce or peanut sauce.

Satay Chicken

Serves: 3-4
Preparation Time: 30 minutes plus 4 hours marinating time
Cooking Time: 8-10 minutes

Ingredients

<u>Peanut-coconut milk sauce</u>
1 tablespoon dark soy sauce
1 small onion, minced
½ cup peanut butter
2 tablespoons brown sugar
1 cup coconut milk
1 teaspoon Sriracha or red pepper flakes, or
to taste Salt, as needed
2 tablespoons peanuts, toasted and crushed
2 teaspoons honey, or to taste (optional)

<u>For satay</u>
2 pounds chicken breast fillets (you may also use pork or beef)

1 tablespoon ground coriander
1 tablespoon curry powder
2 teaspoons cumin powder
½ teaspoon turmeric powder
½ teaspoon pepper
¼ cup sugar
2 teaspoons salt
6 cloves garlic, peeled
¼ cup lemongrass, roughly chopped
¼ cup cilantro, roughly chopped
½ cup coconut milk
3-4 tablespoons condensed milk
1 tablespoon vegetable oil

Directions

For peanut-coconut milk sauce

1. In a saucepan, whisk together all the ingredients EXCEPT the crushed peanuts and honey (optional).
2. Heat over medium-high heat and bring to a boil, stirring or whisking continuously.
3. Remove from the heat.
4. Taste and adjust the flavor with more chili sauce or salt. Add honey, if desired.
5. Add peanuts and mix well. May be used warm or at room temperature.

For satay

6. Trim the chicken and remove any fat or cartilage.
7. Cut the meat into about 2-inch by 1-inch strips.
8. Butterfly the strips by cutting a ¼-inch thick strip horizontally up to about ¼-inch from where the meat is joined. Cut again to lengthen, cutting the thicker portion from the 'joint' outward. So you will have long piece of chicken meat, about 5-6 inches long and ¼-inch thick. Do the same for the rest of the chicken.
9. Place the meat in a bowl and add coriander, curry, cumin, turmeric, and pepper powders. Add the sugar and salt. Mix well

and set aside.

10. In a blender, mix together the garlic, lemongrass, cilantro, and coconut milk. Blend until smooth.
11. Pour the coconut milk mixture over chicken.
12. Add the condensed milk and oil.
13. Mix everything together with your hands until well blended.
14. Cover with plastic wrap, refrigerate and let it marinate for 4 hours to overnight.
15. Using a kitchen knife, cut the edges of the skewered chicken so they don't dangle.
16. Use any leftover marinade as a glaze while grilling.
17. Grill the skewers over medium-low heat for 4-5 minutes on each side, brushing with marinade from time to time. The satay will look dry when it's done.
18. Serve with peanut-coconut milk sauce or peanut dipping sauce and toasted bread, if desired.

Soups

Spicy Lemongrass Soup (Tom Yum)

Serves: 3-4
Preparation Time: 5 minutes
Cooking Time: 30 minutes

Ingredients
1 teaspoon soy sauce
1 teaspoon white sugar
1 teaspoon red curry paste, or to taste
4 cups water
2 stalks of lemon grass, sliced
4-6 kaffir lime leaves
1 bunch Bok choy, leaves separated, each leaf halved
½ cup baby corn, sliced
¼ cup carrot, diced small
1 medium tomato, sliced
3-4 ounces mushrooms, roughly chopped

1 red bell pepper, diced small
2 tablespoons lime juice
Salt to taste
1 tablespoon Thai basil leaves, for garnish

Directions

1. Combine the soy sauce, sugar and red curry paste in a cup or bowl. Set it aside.
2. Heat the water in a saucepan, and add the lemon grass. Tear the lime leaves and drop them into the water.
3. Boil for 5 minutes, until the water has turned green and fragrant.
4. Strain out the lemon grass and lime leaves and return the stock to the saucepan.
5. Add the Bok choy, baby corn, carrot, tomato, mushrooms, and bell pepper.
6. Bring it to a boil. Cook until the vegetables are tender but not overcooked.
7. Add the soy sauce mixture and lime juice.
8. Season with salt and adjust the flavor according to taste. Tom Yum should be sour and spicy. Add more lime juice or red curry paste, as needed.
9. Serve hot, garnished with Thai basil.

Quick Coconut Soup (Tom Kha)

Serves: 2
Preparation Time: 10 minutes
Cooking Time: 10 minutes

Ingredients

1 (14-ounce) can coconut milk
2 cups chicken stock
1 1-inch piece of ginger, peeled and chopped
1 pound shrimp, cleaned, shelled and deveined OR chicken breast, trimmed and sliced OR a combination of both
1 cup mushrooms, cleaned and sliced
2 tablespoons fresh lime juice
Zest of 1 lemon or lime
1 tablespoon fish sauce
1 teaspoon chili paste or Sriracha
For garnish
Green onion, chopped
Cilantro, chopped

Directions

1. Bring the coconut milk, chicken stock and ginger to boil in a pot, then reduce to a simmer.
2. Add the rest of ingredients (except the garnishes) and simmer. Cook for 5 minutes for shrimp, or 10 minutes for chicken. If you're using both, add the chicken and cook for 5 minutes before adding the shrimp and cooking another 5 minutes.
3. Adjust the flavor with more fish sauce and chili or Sriracha, as desired.
4. Serve hot, garnished with green onion and cilantro.

Salads

Papaya Salad (Som Tum)

Serves: 2
Preparation Time: 20 minutes
Cooking Time: 5 minutes or none

Ingredients

2 cups shredded green papaya
2 cloves garlic, peeled
1 tablespoon dried shrimp (optional)
1-3 fresh birds eye chilies
½ piece palm sugar OR 1 tablespoon sugar
½ cup chopped tomato, preferably cherry
1-2 tablespoons green beans, topped and sliced thinly, 1 inch
in length Juice of 1 lime or lemon
1 ½ tablespoons fish sauce
2 tablespoons toasted peanuts, crushed

Directions

1. If using palm sugar, melt it in 2 tablespoons of water in a pan over low heat to make a thick syrup. Set it aside to cool.
2. In a mortar and pestle, crush the garlic and dried shrimp (optional). Follow this with the chili. Crush but do not puree. If your mortar and pestle is large enough, the green papaya and continue pounding to incorporate the flavor. If not, simply mix crushed garlic, shrimp, and chili with the papaya in a bowl.
3. Add the liquid palm sugar (or sugar), tomatoes, beans, lime juice and fish sauce. Mix thoroughly to blend flavors.
4. Sprinkle with crushed peanuts and serve.

Thai BBQ Beef Salad

Serves: 4
Preparation Time: 20 minutes plus 4 hours marinating time
Cooking Time: 10 minutes

Ingredients

1 pound beef steak, sliced about 1 to 1 ½-inches thick

For marinade or dressing (to be divided)
3 tablespoons lime juice, divided
3 tablespoons soy sauce
3 tablespoons vegetable oil
2 tablespoon brown sugar
3 cloves garlic, minced
1 ½ teaspoons ginger, minced
1 ¼ teaspoons red curry paste or chili-garlic sauce

For salad
½ head red-leaf lettuce, torn
½ red bell pepper, trimmed and julienned

½ cucumber, seeded and julienned
½ cup cilantro leaves, rinsed and dried
1 cup chiffonade of basil leaves
3 shallots, thinly sliced, divided, for garnish

Directions

1. Pat the beef dry with paper towels.
2. In a bowl, combine ingredients for marinade/dressing. Mix well to blend the flavors. Divide, and keep half to be used as dressing. Refrigerate.
3. Add the other half to the meat and let marinate in the fridge for 4 hours to overnight.
4. Grill the marinated beef to medium-rare (about 5 minutes on each side) or to desired doneness. Remove it from the heat and let it cool.
5. Slice the meat thinly against the grain.
6. Combine the rest of the ingredients, setting aside some shallots for garnish.
7. Add the dressing and toss the ingredients to coat.
8. Garnish with remaining shallots, and serve.

Thai Tofu and Chicken Salad with Peanut Dressing

Serves: 2
Preparation Time: 5 minutes
Cooking Time: 5-10 minutes

Ingredients

<u>Peanut dressing</u>
3 tablespoons water
2 tablespoons rice wine vinegar
1 tablespoon green onions, chopped
1 tablespoon peanut butter
1 tablespoon soy sauce
1 teaspoon ginger, peeled and grated
1 teaspoon Sriracha or chili sauce
1 teaspoon dark sesame oil
2 teaspoons dry-roasted peanuts

<u>For salad</u>
3 ounces extra-firm tofu
2 cups mixed baby salad greens
½ cup fresh bean sprouts
2 tablespoons red onion, vertically sliced
2 tablespoons fresh mint leaves
2 tablespoons fresh cilantro leaves

1 medium carrot, peeled and julienned
4 cherry tomatoes, quartered
1 cup cooked chicken breast, shredded

Directions

1. Prepare the dressing by first setting aside peanuts and then putting the rest of the ingredients in a blender. Blend until smooth. Add peanuts and blend for about 10 seconds, just to crush peanuts. Or, crush the peanuts beforehand in a mortar and pestle and sprinkle over the dressing. Set aside.
2. Fry the tofu until it is golden brown on all sides. Drain, and cut it into bite-sized pieces. Set it aside. Alternately, you may cut the tofu first before frying, to get a crisper texture.
3. For the salad, mix all the ingredients together. Add the dressing and toss to coat evenly.
4. Sprinkle with fried tofu cubes and serve.

Noodles and Rices

Chicken Pad Thai

Serves: 4
Preparation Time: 10 minutes
Cooking Time: 15 minutes

Ingredients

1 (8-ounce) box pad Thai rice noodles

10 tablespoons pad Thai sauce, store-bought OR make your own

3 tablespoons vegetable oil, divided

3 cloves garlic, minced

1 shallot, finely sliced

8 ounces chicken breast fillet, trimmed and sliced thinly

2 eggs

1 cup bean sprouts

Pad Thai sauce ingredients

3 tablespoons soy sauce

1 tablespoon chili sauce or Sriracha

1 tablespoon tamarind paste OR 2 tablespoons lime juice

1 tablespoon fish sauce

2 tablespoons palm sugar or brown sugar

2 tablespoons vegetable or peanut oil

For garnish

Cilantro, chopped

Lime wedges

Toasted peanuts, crushed

Directions

1. Soak the noodles in hot (not boiling) water for about 10 minutes and drain (or follow the instructions on the package). Set aside.
2. If not using store-bought pad Thai sauce, whisk together the sauce ingredients in a bowl and set aside.
3. Heat a wok over high heat. Add 2 tablespoons of oil and sauté the garlic, shallots, and chicken.
4. Cook until the chicken is done, about 10 minutes. Remove from the wok.
5. Add remaining oil to the wok and scramble the eggs.
6. Reduce the heat and add the pad Thai sauce, then the noodles, and toss to coat evenly.
7. Add the chicken mixture and stir until heated through.
8. Serve with cilantro, peanuts, and lime.

Chicken Pad See Ew

Serves: 3
Preparation Time: 10 minutes
Cooking Time: 5 minutes

Ingredients

1 (8-ounce) pack rice stick noodles or *Sen Yai* Noodles

For sauce

2 tablespoons dark soy sauce (or 1 ½ tablespoons soy sauce + 1 tablespoon honey)
2 tablespoons oyster sauce
2 teaspoons soy sauce
2 teaspoons white vinegar
2 teaspoons sugar
2 tablespoons water

Stir-fry

2 tablespoons peanut or vegetable oil

2 cloves garlic, smashed

1 cup skinless chicken thighs or breast fillet, cut into bite-sized pieces Broccoli stems, julienned

1 large egg

4 cups Chinese broccoli (or you can use Bok choy or pak choy), separate leaves from stems

Directions

1. Soak the noodles in hot (not boiling) water for about 10 minutes and drain (or follow the packaging instructions). Set aside.
2. Combine the sauce ingredients and set aside.
3. Place the smashed garlic in the oil in a wok over high heat. Crush the garlic to mince as the wok heats up.
4. When the oil is hot and garlic is golden brown, add the chicken and broccoli stems. Stir-fry for 1 minute.
5. Push the garlic, broccoli, and chicken to the side of the wok, and scramble the egg in the oil. Expect some charring, which will add flavor.
6. Add the noodles, broccoli leaves, and the sauce.
7. Toss to coat evenly, and continue cooking until the leaves begin to wilt.
8. Remove from the heat and serve.

Drunken Noodles (Pad Kee Mao)

Serves: 2-3
Preparation Time: 10 minutes
Cooking Time: 5 minutes

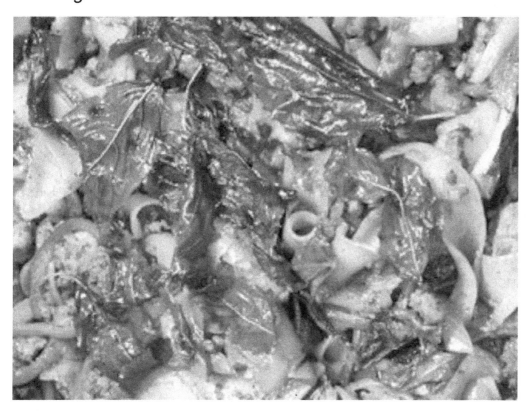

Ingredients

1 (7-ounce) pack pad Thai noodles, dried

For sauce

3 tablespoons oyster sauce
3 tablespoons regular soy sauce (or 1:1 dark to light soy sauce)
2 teaspoons sugar
2 tablespoons water

For stir-fry

2 tablespoons peanut or vegetable oil
3 large cloves garlic, minced
1-3 birds eye chilies, deseeded and very finely chopped
10 ounces chicken thigh or breast fillet, cut into bite-sized pieces
1 cup basil leaves, preferably holy basil (*kaphrao*)

2 shallot stems, cut into 2-inch pieces

½ cup carrot, julienned

½ cup canned bamboo shoots, rinsed and drained (if using pre-cooked, vacuum packed, open pack just before use, rinse and cut)

¼ red bell pepper, deseeded and julienned

Directions

1. Soak the noodles in hot (not boiling) water for about 10 minutes and drain (or follow the packaging instructions). Set aside.
2. Whisk together sauce ingredients in a small bowl and set aside.
3. Heat oil in wok or pan over high heat. Add the garlic and chilies and cook for 10 seconds.
4. Add the chicken and stir-fry until it is done, about 2-3 minutes.
5. Add the shallot stems, carrot, and about 1 tablespoon of sauce, and stir to coat the chicken.
6. Add the noodles, bamboo shoots, bell pepper, and the rest of the sauce, and cook until evenly coated. If the noodles are too dry, add about a tablespoon (or more, if needed) of hot water and stir.
7. Turn off the heat. Add the basil leaves and stir to wilt the leaves in the hot noodles.
8. Serve.

Stir-Fried Glass Noodles (Pad Woon Sen)

Serves: 4
Preparation Time: 20 minutes
Cooking Time: 15 minutes

Ingredients

6 ounces glass or bean noodles (*woon sen*)

For the sauce

3 tablespoons fish sauce
3 tablespoons Sriracha sauce
1 tablespoon oyster sauce
1 tablespoon rice wine vinegar
½ teaspoon sesame oil

For the noodles

3 tablespoons peanut oil, divided
2 eggs
Pinch of salt
1 small yellow onion, julienned
2 stalks celery, sliced thin on the bias
3 garlic cloves, crushed and minced

1 small carrot, peeled and julienned
 2 shallot stems, cut into 2-inch pieces
1 cup Napa cabbage, finely sliced
2 chicken fillets, trimmed and cut into very thin strips

Directions

1. Soak the noodles in hot (not boiling) water for about 10 minutes (or follow the packaging instructions). Drain, and set aside.
2. Add a pinch of salt to the eggs and beat thoroughly.
3. In a small bowl, whisk together the sauce ingredients and set that aside.
4. Heat a wok over medium heat. Add 2 tablespoons of peanut oil and swirl to coat the pan.
5. Add the beaten eggs and let them cook for about 1 minute. Transfer the cooked eggs to a cutting board and slice them into ribbons. Set aside.
6. In the same wok, add about a teaspoon more of oil and heat almost to the smoking point.
7. Sauté the onion until translucent. Add the celery and stir-fry for 30 seconds.
8. Add the garlic and stir-fry for 15 seconds.
9. Add another teaspoon of oil to the wok, if needed. Add the carrot and shallots and stir-fry for about 1 minute.
10. Add the Napa cabbage and cook until it begins to wilt. Remove this mixture of vegetables from the wok and transfer it to a dish.
11. To the same wok, add remaining oil as needed. Allow it to heat up for about 15 seconds and then add chicken slices. Stir-fry until the chicken is done.
12. Add the drained noodles and about 2/3 of the sauce. Toss and continue cooking until the noodles are well coated, the liquid has been absorbed. Adjust saltiness, if needed.
13. Transfer the noodle and chicken mixture to a serving dish. Pour in the remaining sauce, vegetables, and egg ribbons. Toss to coat evenly.
14. Serve.

Thai Fried Rice

Serves: 4-6
Preparation Time: 5 minutes
Cooking Time: 15-20 minutes

Ingredients

4 cups precooked cold jasmine rice

3-4 tablespoons peanut oil or vegetable oil

4 cloves garlic, minced

1 ½ cups boneless skinless chicken breast fillets (lean pork or beef may be used), thinly sliced

2 eggs, beaten and seasoned with salt and pepper

¾ cup snow peas, trimmed

½ cup carrot, julienned

4 green onions, sliced thin

1 tomato, chopped

2 teaspoons palm sugar or table sugar

3 tablespoons Thai fish sauce

1 tablespoon oyster sauce

1-3 teaspoons chili sauce, or according to taste

For garnish
½ cup cilantro, chopped
1 cucumber, sliced
2 limes, cut into wedges

Directions

1. Break up the cold rice with a wooden spoon or your hands (this is better) to separate the grains. Use plastic gloves or wet your hands so the rice does not stick. Set it aside.
2. Heat a large wok or large nonstick skillet over medium-high heat.
3. Add the oil and swirl, then add the garlic and stir-fry for about 30 seconds.
4. Add chicken slices and stir-fry until done.
5. Move to the side of the wok and add more oil, if needed. Allow the oil to heat up again for about 15 seconds.
6. Pour in the beaten egg and scramble.
7. Add the snow peas and carrots, and stir-fry for about 45 seconds.
8. Add the rice, constantly scooping from the bottom up to ensure even frying. You should smell the rice getting toasted.
9. Add the spring onions, tomato, sugar, and sauces. Continue stir-frying to coat the rice with flavor.
10. Serve garnished with the cilantro, cucumbers, and lime wedges, with fish and chili sauces on the side.

Pineapple Fried Rice

Serves: 5
Preparation Time: 30 minutes
Cooking Time: 10 minutes

Ingredients

4 cups cold, precooked rice
2-3 tablespoons peanut or vegetable oil, divided
2 shallots, finely chopped

3 cloves garlic, finely chopped
1 red or green chili, thinly sliced
2-4 tablespoons vegetable or chicken stock
2 eggs, beaten and seasoned with salt and
pepper ½ cup frozen peas (optional)
1 small carrot, julienned (optional)
1 ½ cups pineapple chunks, canned or fresh,
drained ¼ cup raisins
½ cup roasted, unsalted whole cashew nuts

For sauce
1 tablespoon fish sauce
2 tablespoons soy sauce
2 teaspoons curry powder
½ teaspoon sugar

For garnish
3 stalks spring onion, chopped
⅓ cup fresh cilantro, chopped

Directions

1. Break up the cold rice with a wooden spoon or your hands (this is better) to separate the grains. Use plastic gloves or wet your hands so the rice does not stick. Set it aside.
2. Combine the sauce ingredients in a small bowl or cup. Set them aside.
3. Heat up a large wok or non-stick skillet over medium-high heat.
4. Add 2 tablespoons of oil.
5. Sauté the shallots, garlic, and chili for about 1 minute or until fragrant. Add 1 tablespoon of stock to sizzle and deglaze. Push it to the side of the wok.
6. Add the beaten eggs to the center of the wok and scramble.
7. Peas and carrots (if using) may be added at this point. Stock may be added a tablespoon at a time to prevent the mixture from drying out, if needed. Stir-fry for 1 minute.
8. Add about a tablespoon more of oil, if needed, and allow to heat up.

9. Add the rice, pineapple chunks, raisins, and cashew nuts.
10. Add the prepared sauce and gently stir-fry to combine over medium-high to high heat. "Shovel" the rice with a spatula from the bottom up constantly. The rice should make gentle popping sounds, about 5 minutes.
11. Adjust the flavor with a little salt or chili sauce, as desired. If necessary, the saltiness can be reduced with a few drops of lime juice.
12. This dish is traditionally served in a carved-out pineapple. Garnish with cilantro and spring onion.

Chicken and Duck Main Entrées

Easy Chicken Coconut Green Curry

Serves: 8
Preparation Time: 5 minutes (does not include curry paste preparation)
Cooking Time: 15 minutes

Ingredients

Green Curry Paste
4-6 green chilies, seeded and chopped
2 shallots, chopped
1 tablespoon ginger, peeled and grated
2 cloves garlic, crushed
1 bunch cilantro
2 stalks lemongrass, bruised
Zest of 1 lime
Juice of 1 lime
8 kaffir lime leaves, torn
1 tablespoon galangal, peeled and chopped

1 tablespoon coriander seeds, crushed

1 teaspoon ground cumin

1 teaspoon black peppercorns, crushed

2 teaspoon fish sauce

4 tablespoons peanut or vegetable oil

For curry

2 tablespoons vegetable oil

2-3 tablespoons green curry paste (homemade or store-bought)

1 ½ pounds boneless chicken thigh or breast fillet, cut into 1-inch pieces

3 cups coconut cream or coconut milk (about 2 cans)

1 cup string beans, topped and cut into 1 ½- to 2-inch

pieces ½ medium carrot, peeled and thinly sliced

4 ounces bamboo shoot, canned or vacuum packed, drained and sliced

1 medium Japanese eggplant, cut into 2-inch pieces

½ cup mixed bell peppers (red and green), seeded and cut into

bite-size pieces

1 tablespoon fish sauce, or to taste

1 teaspoon sugar, or to taste

Soy sauce, to taste (optional)

Directions

For green curry paste

Note: Use rubber gloves when handling chili peppers to avoid pepper burns.

1. Pound or mash the lemongrass in a mortar and pestle, and then blend it with all the other ingredients in a food processor. Store it in a glass jar, and refrigerate.

For curry

2. Heat the oil in large wok, pot, or Dutch oven over medium heat.
3. Fry the curry paste until fragrant (about 2 minutes). Be careful not to inhale the vapors or smoke, as they can cause coughing.
4. Stir in the chicken slices and cook for about 5 minutes, allowing the chicken to absorb the curry flavor.
5. Add the coconut cream or milk and cook for 10-15 minutes, or until the chicken is done and you begin to see oil separated from

the coconut cream floating on the surface.

6. Add the vegetables and cook about 5 minutes more, or until the vegetables are cooked to the desired tenderness and the sauce has thickened.

7. Adjust the flavor with fish sauce, sugar, and soy sauce (optional). If more curry flavor is needed, sauté more curry paste in a small amount of oil before adding to the stew.

8. Serve with rice.

Red Curry with Chicken

Serves: 2
Preparation Time: 5 minutes (does not include curry paste preparation)
Cooking Time: 15 minutes

Ingredients

Red Curry Paste

15-20 dried hot red chilies (*prik haeng*), seeded and chopped
4 teaspoons coriander seeds
2 stalks fresh lemongrass, outer leaves removed
1 teaspoon black peppercorns
4 teaspoons galangal, peeled and chopped
6 kaffir lime leaves, finely chopped
2 tablespoons cilantro roots or stems, chopped
5 small shallots, chopped
¼ cup garlic, chopped
15-20 fresh red bird's-eye chilies (*prik kii noo*), finely chopped
2 teaspoons Thai shrimp paste (*kapi*)
½ teaspoon salt

For curry

1 ½ tablespoons peanut or vegetable oil
2-3 tablespoons red curry paste (homemade or store-bought), or to taste
8 ounces chicken breast, cut into bite-sized pieces (you may also use beef, pork or shrimp)
½ cup coconut milk
½ cup chicken stock or water
½ medium carrot, peeled and sliced thinly
4 ounces bamboo shoot, canned or vacuum packed, drained and sliced
1 medium Japanese eggplant, cut into 2-inch pieces
5 kaffir lime leaves, lightly bruised
2 pieces red chili, cut into thick strips
1 tablespoon fish sauce
1 teaspoon sugar or palm sugar, or to taste ¼ cup Thai basil leaves
½ small green bell pepper, seeded and cut into bite-size pieces (optional)
½ small red bell pepper, seeded and cut into bite-size pieces (optional)

Directions

For red curry paste

Note: Use rubber gloves when handling chili peppers to avoid pepper burns.

1. Soak the dried, chopped chilies in water for about 20 minutes. Drain well.
2. Heat a skillet over medium heat, and toast the coriander until fragrant, about 3 minutes.
3. Bash the coriander and peppercorns in the mortar and pestle, and set aside.
4. Slice the lemongrass stalks thinly and bruise them in a mortar and pestle.
5. Combine the lemongrass, galangal, lime leaves, cilantro, shallots, garlic, fresh chilies, and soaked dried chilies in a bowl. Add the shrimp paste and salt. In 3 batches, blend the mixture in a food processor, adding 1 ½ tablespoons of water per batch, to form a smooth paste.
6. Add the shrimp paste and salt, and pulse to blend.
7. Store it in small glass jars. Keep refrigerated.

For curry

8. Heat up a wok or pot over medium heat and add the oil.
9. Sauté the red curry paste until fragrant.
10. Stir in the chicken, mixing well to ensure absorption of the curry flavor.
11. Pour in coconut milk and water or stock, and bring to a quick boil, about 2 minutes.
12. Add the carrot, beans, bamboo shoots, eggplant, kaffir lime leaves, and red chili.
13. Reduce the heat. Cover the pot and let it simmer until the sauce begins to thicken, about 10 minutes.
14. Add the fish sauce, sugar, basil leaves, and bell peppers (optional). Stir.
15. Adjust flavor with fish sauce, sugar, and soy sauce (optional). If more curry flavor is needed, sauté more curry paste in a small amount of oil before adding it to the stew.
16. Serve with rice.

Panang Curry with Chicken

Serves: 4

Preparation Time: 15 minutes plus 30 minutes preparation of homemade Panang curry paste

Cooking Time: 20 minutes

Ingredients

<u>Panang Curry Paste</u>

2 tablespoons lemongrass, sliced thin

1 tablespoon coriander seeds, toasted

½ teaspoon cumin seeds, toasted

2 tablespoons black peppercorns, crushed

1 tablespoon galangal, peeled and chopped

6 kaffir lime leaves, chopped

2 tablespoons cilantro root, peeled and chopped

1 teaspoon salt

2 shallots, sliced thin

5 cloves garlic, chopped

1 teaspoon shrimp paste

4 pieces of mace, toasted

2 cardamom pods, toasted

4 large green peppers, roasted

10 big red dried chilies, soaked in water for 10 minutes.

For curry

2-3 tablespoons Panang curry paste (homemade or store-bought), or according to taste

2-3 tablespoons peanut or vegetable oil

4 cups coconut milk

⅔ pound boneless, skinless, chicken breast, cubed

1 cup string beans, topped and cut into 1 ½- to 2-inch pieces ½ cup carrot, peeled and sliced thinly

2 tablespoons palm sugar (you may use coconut sugar, muscovado, or table sugar)

2 tablespoons fish sauce, or to taste

6 kaffir lime leaves, torn

½ cup red and green bell pepper slices, chopped

For garnish

2 pieces red chili peppers, sliced

¼ cup fresh Thai basil leaves

Directions

For Panang curry paste

1. Pound first 4 ingredients in a mortar and pestle one at a time.
2. Combine everything in a food processor and blend to make a smooth paste. You may also pound everything, adding ingredients one at a time in a large mortar and pestle, but the resulting flavor is better than when using a food processor. Note: Use rubber gloves when handling chili peppers to avoid pepper burns.
3. Store in glass jars and refrigerate.

For curry

4. Heat up a wok or pot over medium heat, and add the oil.
5. Sauté the Panang curry paste until fragrant.
6. Stir in the coconut milk and bring it to a boil, about 2 minutes.

7. Add the chicken and cook, with frequent stirring, until chicken is done, about 10-15 minutes.
8. Add the string beans, carrot, sugar, fish sauce, kaffir lime leaves, and bell pepper.
9. Reduce the heat. Cover the pot and let it simmer until the sauce begins to thicken, about 5 minutes.
10. Adjust the flavor according to taste with more fish sauce, if necessary.
11. Remove from heat, and garnish with chili and Thai basil.
12. Serve with rice.

Jungle Curry

Serves: 4
Preparation Time: 8 minutes
Cooking Time: 20 minutes

Ingredients

1 cup water or chicken stock
1-3 tablespoons <u>red curry paste</u> (homemade or store-bought), or according to taste
1 1-inch piece fresh galangal, peeled and sliced or grated
1 teaspoon rhizome (optional), skin scraped off and thinly sliced
1 pound chicken thighs or breast fillet, thinly sliced
2 tablespoons fish sauce
1 teaspoon sugar
½ medium carrot, peeled and thinly sliced
½ cup bamboo shoots (canned or vacuum-packed), drained and sliced
½ cup canned baby corn, halved horizontally
½ cup canned straw mushrooms, sliced
8-10 string beans, cut into 2-inch pieces
½ cup green and/or red bell peppers, seeded and cut into bite-size pieces

6 kaffir leaves

1 bunch Napa cabbage, washed and leaves separated

15 basil leaves

Directions

1. In a wok or pot, combine the water, red curry paste, galangal, and rhizome (optional).
2. Bring the mixture to a boil, add the chicken, and simmer for 10 minutes.
3. Stir in the fish sauce, sugar, carrot, bamboo shoots, baby corn, straw mushrooms, string beans, bell peppers, and kaffir leaves.
4. Cover and bring again to a boil. Reduce the heat and let it simmer for 5 minutes.
5. Add the Napa cabbage and basil leaves, and cook for 2 more minutes.
6. Serve with rice.

Tamarind Duck

Serves: 2-3
Preparation Time: 5 minutes plus 30 minutes marinating time and 10 minutes soaking time (optional)
Cooking Time: 15-20 minutes

Ingredients
2 duck breasts, skin on, boneless

For marinade
1 star anise, toasted
2 cinnamon sticks, toasted
4 cloves garlic
1 cilantro root
1 teaspoon white pepper powder
1 tablespoon light soy sauce
1 tablespoon oil

For sauce
1 cilantro root

3 cloves garlic

1 star anise, toasted

1 teaspoon white pepper powder

1 tablespoon vegetable oil

2 cinnamon sticks, toasted

1 cup chicken stock

1 ½ tablespoons palm sugar (or muscovado, coconut, or table sugar)

1 teaspoon honey

1 teaspoon dark soy sauce

2 teaspoons light soy sauce

1 ½ teaspoons fish sauce

½ cup tamarind sauce (homemade or store-
bought) Chili paste or sauce, to taste

4 Chinese/shiitake mushrooms, rehydrated and halved (optional)

1 cup chestnuts (optional)

For steamed vegetables

Steamed baby Bok choy, bell pepper, broccoli, and baby corn
(or any vegetable of choice)

For garnish

3-4 Thai chilies

Cilantro

Fried onion flakes (optional)

Directions

1. Wipe the duck breasts dry with paper towels and cut several slits on the flesh for better absorption of the marinade.
2. Toast the cinnamon sticks and star anise in a hot wok or skillet for about 30 seconds.
3. If using dried mushrooms, soak them in hot water for 10-20 minutes and halve. Set them aside.

For marinade

4. Pound the star anise, cinnamon sticks, garlic, and cilantro in a mortar and pestle to make a coarse paste.
5. Add the white pepper, soy sauce, and oil to the paste and rub this

all over the duck breasts.

6. Cover and let marinate for at least 30 minutes (the longer the better).
7. Bake the marinated duck at 300°F for 25-35 minutes or until the surface is well browned and the flesh is no longer pink.
8. Transfer to serving dish.

For sauce

9. Pound the cilantro, garlic, star anise and white pepper in a mortar and pestle to make a paste.
10. Heat a wok or skillet over medium heat and then add the oil.
11. Sauté the paste in the oil until fragrant.
12. Add the cinnamon sticks, chicken stock, palm sugar, honey, soy sauces, fish sauce, tamarind sauce, and chili sauce. Stir and cook for about 1 minute.
13. Add mushrooms and chestnuts (optional).
14. Continue cooking until thickened.
15. Adjust the saltiness, sweetness, or spiciness, as desired. Remove the cinnamon sticks, and pour the mixture over the roasted duck breasts.
16. Serve with steamed vegetables and garnish with Thai chilies, cilantro, and fried onion flakes (optional).

Pork Main Entrées

Thai Lemongrass Pork Chops

Serves: 4
Preparation Time: 5 minutes plus 2 hours marinating time
Cooking Time: 10-15 minutes

Ingredients

4 pork chops, about ¾ inch thick, rinsed and drained Lemon zest or cilantro (for garnish)

For marinade
2 cloves garlic, minced
2 stalks lemongrass, thinly sliced
1 teaspoon cracked black pepper
2 tablespoons brown sugar
2 tablespoons fish sauce
1 teaspoon dark sesame oil

1 tablespoon rice wine

Directions

1. Dry the pork chops with paper towels, and set them aside.
2. Pound or bash the garlic, lemongrass, and black pepper in a mortar and pestle. Transfer it to a bowl.
3. Add the rest of marinade ingredients and mix well. Pour it over the pork.
4. Let pork chops marinate for 2 hours to overnight, refrigerated.
5. Let the chops warm to room temperature, and preheat the grill to about 450°F.
6. Brush the pork chops with oil and grill for 5-7 minutes on each side.
7. Garnish with lemon zest and serve with steamed vegetables (broccoli, baby corn, Bok choy, carrot, etc.), if desired.

Thai Barbecue Pork

Serves: 4
Preparation Time: 5 minutes plus 15 minutes marinating time
Cooking Time: 15 minutes

Ingredients

1 pound pork tenderloin, cut into ½-inch slices

Cilantro or Thai sweet basil (for garnish)

<u>For marinade</u>

1 stalk fresh lemongrass, stem and coarse leaves trimmed, cut into chunks, bruised

1 tablespoon sugar

2 tablespoons soy sauce

1 tablespoon fish sauce

1 thumb (1-inch piece) fresh ginger, peeled and sliced ¼ teaspoon pepper

1 tablespoon Thai <u>red curry paste</u>

2 cloves garlic, peeled

2 tablespoons vegetable oil

Directions

1. Dry pork using paper towels. Set aside.
2. Place marinade ingredients in a blender or food processor and make a paste, adding some water if too dry.
3. Preheat grill to 450°F.
4. Marinate the pork in the marinade for 15 minutes.
5. Grill for 5-7 minutes on each side.
6. Garnish with cilantro or Thai sweet basil, and serve with chili sauce and sticky rice.

Thai Spare Ribs with Tamarind

Serves: 4
Preparation Time: 1 hour and 35 minutes preparation a day before.
Cooking Time: 10 minutes

Ingredients

1-1 ½ pounds pork spareribs
10 kaffir lime leaves
½ cup galangal, skin scraped off and chopped
6 lemongrass stalks, bruised
10 black peppercorns
5 cilantro roots
5 cloves garlic
⅔ cup oyster sauce
½ cup palm sugar
5 tablespoons tamarind paste
Coriander sprigs for garnish

Directions

1. Put the ribs in a pot and add water to cover.
2. Add the kaffir lime, galangal, and lemongrass.
3. Bring to a boil then reduce heat and simmer for 1 ½ hours, or until

the pork is tender and no longer pink. Drain (you may save the stock to use in other dishes) and allow it to cool down.

4. Pound or bash the peppercorns, coriander roots, and garlic in a mortar and pestle to make a paste.
5. Rub the paste over the ribs, cover, and let them marinate in the refrigerator overnight.
6. When the ribs are ready, remove them from the refrigerator and allow them to warm to room temperature.
7. In a saucepan, mix the oyster sauce, palm sugar, and tamarind paste together and bring them to a gentle boil. Reduce the heat and cook until the sauce has thickened.
8. Add the ribs to the sauce, and mix to coat.
9. Grill the ribs until slightly charred (about 5 minutes). Another variation is to grill the ribs first and then glaze the ribs with the sauce.
10. Serve with coriander and chili or Sriracha sauce.

Beef Main Entrées

Massaman Beef Curry

Serves: 8
Preparation Time: 5 minutes plus 40 minutes preparation of homemade massaman curry paste
Cooking Time: 35-40 minutes

Ingredients

<u>Massaman Curry Paste</u>
3 shallots, whole and unpeeled
1 head garlic, whole and unpeeled
4-6 dried whole chilies
1 stalk lemongrass, (only lower half with stem and root) thinly sliced
½ inch piece galangal, julienned
4 pods cardamom
2 1-inch pieces cinnamon stick
5 cloves

1 tablespoon coriander

⅓ tablespoon cumin

⅓ tablespoon peppercorns

1 tablespoon salt

1 mace

1 nutmeg

1 teaspoon shrimp paste

For curry

1 ¼ pounds round or topside steak

Salt and pepper

2-3 tablespoons vegetable oil, divided

2 cloves garlic, crushed

2 ½ to 4 tablespoons massaman curry paste (homemade or store -bought), according to taste

1 (14-ounce) can coconut milk or cream

1 cup beef stock

2 teaspoons palm sugar (or coconut or muscovado sugar)

2 large potatoes, peeled and cut into bite-sized pieces

1 large carrot, cut into chunks

2 teaspoons fish sauce, or to taste

Small handful of fresh basil leaves.

½ cup peanuts, roasted

Basil leaves (for garnish)

Directions

For paste

Note: Use rubber gloves when handling chili peppers to avoid pepper burns

1. Roast the shallots and garlic over direct heat or low flame until the skin is charred and the inside is soft (about 5-10 minutes). Let them cool and then remove the skin. Set aside (You will need these at the last step in making the paste).
2. Remove the stems and seeds from chilies. Chop roughly.
3. In a wok or skillet, toast the chilies and lemongrass by stirring over medium heat until slightly browned, about 2 minutes, until they are fragrant. Remove them from the skillet or wok.
4. Put the remaining paste ingredients, EXCEPT the shrimp paste, in

the wok and toast them for a few seconds.

5. Place the chilies in a mortar and pestle and add the salt. Pound until the chilies are roughly broken.
6. Add the lemongrass and pound. Add the rest of the spices and continue pounding until a coarse paste results. This will take about 30 minutes. A food processor or blender may be used, but pounding is said to release more flavor from the ingredients.
7. Add the roasted shallots and ginger and pound to a smooth paste.
8. Lastly, add the shrimp paste and pound until well blended. The result should be a dark red, fragrant paste.
9. Transfer to a jar and refrigerate. Will keep, refrigerated, for 1 month.

For curry

10. Preheat oven to 350°F.
11. Slice the steaks across the grain to make ½-inch wide strips (this kind of cut will help reduce cooking time). Season with salt and pepper. Drizzle with 1 tablespoon of oil, and mix well.
12. Heat a wok over medium-high heat. Add 1-2 tablespoons of oil, and working in batches, sear and stir-fry the beef in the hot oil. Use a slotted spoon to drain the oil back into the wok while transferring the beef to an oven-proof casserole dish or Dutch oven.
13. Sauté the garlic until fragrant (about 30 seconds). Reduce heat.
14. Add curry paste and continue sautéing for 2 more minutes.
15. Add the coconut milk, beef stock, and sugar. Stir, and bring it to a boil.
16. Add the potatoes, carrot, fish sauce, and the small handful of basil leaves. Simmer for about a minute.
17. Transfer this mixture to the casserole dish or Dutch oven where the beef is, and mix well.
18. Cover and place it in the oven.
19. Bake for 30 minutes. The beef and potatoes should be tender.
20. Sprinkle with roasted peanuts and garnish with basil leaves. Serve with rice.

Yellow Curry with Beef

Serves: 4

Preparation Time: 5 minutes plus 1 hour preparation of homemade curry paste

Cooking Time: 30 minutes

Ingredients

Yellow curry paste

4 large shallots, whole and peeled
4 large heads of garlic, whole, outer skin removed
½ cup fresh ginger, peeled and
sliced 5-20 whole dried Thai chilies
1 ½ tablespoons salt
2-3 tablespoons turmeric powder
2-3 tablespoons mild curry powder
2 teaspoons roasted ground coriander
3 tablespoons lemongrass paste
¼ cup cilantro leaves and stems, packed

For curry

⅔-1 pound beef steak, cut into thin, bite-sized
pieces 1 tablespoon vegetable oil
2 ½ tablespoons yellow curry paste (homemade or store-bought), or to taste
1 small onion, minced
1 (14-ounce) can coconut milk
1 medium potato, peeled and cut into bite-size pieces
1 medium carrot, peeled and sliced
2 plum tomatoes, cut into wedges
2 teaspoons fish sauce
Juice of ½ lime
Cilantro, chopped (for garnish)

Directions

For yellow curry paste
Note: Use rubber gloves when handling chili peppers to avoid pepper burns

1. Preheat the oven to 350°F.
2. Do not separate the garlic into cloves. Slice off the pointy tops but leave the heads whole.
3. Drizzle the shallots, garlic, and ginger with oil.
4. Wrap the shallots and garlic separately in foil.
5. Arrange the ginger slices in a layer and wrap with foil.
6. Place on a baking sheet and bake for 15 minutes. Remove the ginger as it should already be tender.
7. Turn up the oven temperature to 400°F and continue roasting the

shallots and garlic for 30 minutes or until golden brown and fragrant.
8. Meanwhile, soak the dried chilies in water for 15 minutes to rehydrate. Drain.
9. Place all the paste ingredients in a food processor or blender and process to make a paste. Keep refrigerated in glass jars.

For curry

10. Heat a saucepan or wok over medium heat and add the oil.
11. Stir-fry the curry paste until fragrant.
12. Add the beef and onion, and mix well to coat with curry paste. Cook until the meat is no longer pink.
13. Stir in the coconut milk and bring it to a boil.
14. Reduce heat and simmer for 15 minutes. Beef should be tender.
15. Add potatoes and carrots and simmer another 15 minutes or until the vegetables are tender.
16. Add the tomatoes, fish sauce, and lime juice. Stir well to combine, and remove from the heat.
17. Garnish with coriander and serve with rice.

Beef Peanut Curry

Serves: 2-3
Preparation Time: 5 minutes
Cooking Time: 20-30 minutes

Ingredients

1 pound steak, cut into bite-sized pieces or
strips Salt and pepper
2-3 tablespoons peanut or vegetable oil
3 cloves garlic, minced
2 teaspoons red curry paste (or to taste)
1 small carrot, peeled and sliced thinly
1 cup potatoes, sliced
1 cup coconut milk
1 tablespoon peanut butter
½ cup red and green bell peppers (mixed), cut in bite-size pieces

Roasted peanuts (for garnish)

Directions

1. Dry the beef with paper towels and season with salt and pepper.
2. Heat up a wok or heavy skillet over medium-high heat. Add the oil.
3. Sear the meat on both sides, remove from the wok, and set aside.
4. Using the same wok with any leftover oil (add more if needed), sauté the garlic and curry paste until fragrant.
5. Stir-fry the carrot and potatoes. The carrot should darken in color and the potatoes should have some brown spots. Add about 1 tablespoon of water, if mixture becomes too dry, and to prevent scorching. Reduce the heat.
6. Stir in the coconut milk and peanut butter. Mix well and cook for about 5 minutes or until the sauce has thickened.
7. Add the seared beef pieces and continue simmering until beef as well as the vegetables are tender.
8. Add the bell peppers and simmer 1 minute longer.
9. Sprinkle with roasted peanuts and serve with rice.

Seafood Main Entrées

Salmon Teriyaki

Serves: 4
Preparation Time: 10 minutes
Cooking Time: 20 minutes

Ingredients

4 boneless, skinless salmon fillets
2 cloves garlic, grated and pounded to a paste
1 thumb (1-inch piece) fresh root ginger, peeled and finely grated
5 tablespoon soy sauce
5 tablespoon *mirin* (rice wine) or dry sherry
1 tablespoon golden caster sugar
1 tablespoon sunflower oil

Directions

1. Wipe the salmon fillet dry with paper towels.
2. In a mortar and pestle, pound the garlic and ginger into a paste.

3. Transfer the paste to a bowl and add soy sauce, mirin, and sugar. Whisk to blend and to dissolve sugar.
4. Preheat a grill or heavy skillet. Coat or brush the skillet with oil.
5. Dip the salmon in the sauce just to coat. Transfer the rest of the sauce mix to a sauce pan and bring to a simmer.
6. While simmering the sauce, grill the salmon over medium-low heat for 20 minutes, brushing occasionally with the sauce. Continue simmering the sauce until thickened and sticky.
7. Turn the salmon over, for even cooking. Remove from the grill when done and transfer to serving dish.
8. Pour the thickened sauce over the salmon and serve.

Seafood Stir-Fry with Basil

Serves: 4
Preparation Time: 5 minutes
Cooking Time: 8- 10 minutes

Ingredients

1 pound mixed seafood (mussels, shrimp, scallops, calamari);
cleaned, shelled, deveined, sliced (for calamari)
3 tablespoons peanut oil
3 cloves garlic, minced
½ red and green bell pepper; cut in bite-sized pieces
½ white onion, minced
2 scallions, white part chopped; green part sliced into 1-inch long pieces
3-4 Thai chilies, chopped
2 tablespoons oyster sauce
1 tablespoon fish sauce
1 teaspoon sugar (preferably palm sugar)
¼ teaspoon ground white pepper
¼ cup chicken stock (omit if you prefer a drier sauce)
1 cup Thai holy basil; washed, dried, and stemmed

Directions

1. Heat a wok or skillet over high heat. Swirl in the oil and heat

almost to the smoking point.

2. Add the garlic and stir for about 30 seconds.
3. Add the bell pepper, white onion, the white parts of the scallions, and the chilies. Cook for 10 seconds.
4. Add the seafood and stir-fry until the shrimp turns pink.
5. Add the sauces, sugar, pepper, stock, and the green part of the scallions, and bring the mixture to a boil. Cook for about 5 minutes.
6. Stir in the basil and cook for 20 seconds, or until the leaves are wilted.
7. Serve hot with rice or noodles.

Vegetarian Main Entrées

Thai Mushrooms and Eggplant Stir-Fry

Serves: 4
Preparation Time: 5 minutes
Cooking Time: 15 minutes

Ingredients

2 pounds Japanese eggplant, cut into bite-sized pieces
3 tablespoons vegetable oil
1 tablespoon minced garlic
1 teaspoon ground chili paste
2 tablespoons minced fresh ginger
½ small yellow onion, cut into thin wedges
2 cups mixed mushrooms, sliced
½ cup carrots, julienned or spiralized
2 tablespoons soy sauce
2 tablespoons vegetarian oyster sauce or
mushroom sauce ½ cup water

¼ cup fresh Thai basil leaves,
halved Rice for serving

Directions

1. Soak the cut eggplant in water to prevent browning or darkening of color. Drain and pat dry with paper towels when ready to cook.
2. Heat a large wok or skillet over medium heat.
3. Swirl in the oil and then add the garlic, chili paste, and ginger. Stir for 30 seconds or until fragrant.
4. Add the drained eggplant and stir-fry for 3 minutes.
5. Add the onion, mushrooms, carrots, soy sauce, and vegetarian oyster sauce. Toss to blend.
6. Reduce the heat and let it simmer for 5 more minutes.
7. Stir in the water one tablespoon at a time.
8. Cook until sauce is just thick enough to coat a spoon.
9. Add the basil and remove from heat.
10. Serve with rice.

Steamed Mixed Vegetables and Tofu

Serves: 4-6
Preparation Time: 5 minutes
Cooking Time: 10 minutes

Ingredients

2 large broccoli crowns, cut into bite-sized pieces
1 cup green beans or string beans, topped and cut into 1 ½-inch pieces
2 stalks lemongrass, cut in half and bruised (optional)
1 medium carrot, peeled and sliced
½ cup mixed (red or green) bell peppers, cut into bite-sized pieces
1 to 2 pieces Thai chili, seeded and finely
chopped 2 scallions, cut into 1-inch long pieces
1 (8-ounce) package baked tofu, cut into bite-size
pieces Salt, to taste

Directions

1. Place the broccoli florets and beans in a wok or stir-fry pan.
2. Add just enough water to keep the bottom of the pan moist.

3. Spread the bruised lemongrass leaves over the vegetables.
4. Cover and steam until the broccoli and beans begin to turn bright green (about 5 minutes).
5. Add the carrot, bell pepper, chilies, scallions, and tofu. Stir.
6. Cover and continue steaming (about 3 minutes) until the vegetables are all tender-crisp. Season with salt.
7. Serve with peanut-coconut milk sauce on the side, and rice.

Vegetable Stir Fry with Green Curry Paste

Serves: 4
Preparation Time: 30 minutes
Cooking Time: 12-15 minutes

Ingredients

½-1 cup cashew nuts
1 ½ cup firm tofu
2 tablespoons vegetable oil
1 clove garlic, minced
3-4 tablespoons green curry paste, or to taste
1 large onion chopped
¼ cup vegetable stock
2 cups broccoli florets
1 bell pepper, trimmed and diced roughly
1 carrot, peeled and sliced thinly

1 cup zucchini, thinly sliced
½ cup pineapple chunks
2 tablespoons oyster sauce
1 tablespoon soy sauce
½ teaspoon sugar
Cilantro leaves, to garnish (optional)

Directions

1. Toast the cashew nuts in an oven at 350-425° by spreading them on a baking sheet and baking for about 5 minutes. Or, toast them on the stovetop in a skillet with about a teaspoon oil. Heat over medium heat and toss for about 5 minutes. Set aside.
2. Wrap the tofu in towels and press down with a weight for about 30 minutes (optional, but this will make the tofu tastier). Wipe dry and cut into 1-inch squares. Roast in a non-stick pan or deep fry (you may fry whole and do the cutting after frying). Drain on paper towels and set aside.
3. Heat a wok over high heat. Swirl in the oil and sauté the garlic, green curry paste and onion until fragrant.
4. Add stock and vegetables, pineapple, sauces, and sugar. Stir-fry until the vegetables are crisp-tender.
5. Stir in the tofu, broccoli, zucchini, peppers, carrot, and cashews, and spring onions and cook about 1 minute more.
6. Remove from the heat and serve garnished with cilantro.

Desserts

Sweet Sticky Rice

Serves: 4
Preparation Time: 10 minutes plus 1 hour
Cooking Time: 20 minutes

Ingredients

1 ½ cups uncooked Thai sticky rice
2 cups water
1 ½ cups coconut milk
1 cup white sugar
½ teaspoon salt

For sauce

½ cup coconut milk
1 tablespoon white sugar
¼ teaspoon salt
1 tablespoon tapioca starch

<u>Accompaniment and topping</u>
3 mangos, peeled and sliced
1 tablespoon toasted sesame seeds

Directions

1. Soak the sticky rice in enough water to cover, for 30 minutes to 1 hour. Drain.
2. Transfer the rice to a rice cooker, add 2 cups of water, and leave it to cook.
3. If you're cooking the rice manually; bring it to a boil and then cover and reduce the heat to low. Simmer over very low heat for 15 to 20 minutes, or until the rice has absorbed all the water.
4. While the rice is cooking, whisk the coconut milk, sugar, and salt in a saucepan and it bring to a boil. Remove from the heat.
5. As soon as rice is cooked, gradually add the coconut milk mixture into the hot rice, stirring, until the rice has absorbed the sauce. You may not have to use all the sauce. Cover and let it sit until cooled and more pudding-like in consistency, about 30 minutes to 1 hour.
6. Meanwhile, prepare the sauce by mixing the sauce ingredients together in a saucepan. Bring it to a boil while whisking. Remove from the heat and set aside.
7. Arrange some of the sliced mango on a serving dish, with a cupful of the sticky rice. Pour the sauce on top and sprinkle with toasted sesame seeds.

Banana Fritters

Serves: 2-4
Preparation Time: 5 minutes
Cooking Time: 5-10 minutes

Ingredients

4 ripe bananas (plantain bananas are also good), peeled and sliced lengthwise

For batter
1 cup plus 2 tablespoons rice flour
1 ½ teaspoon baking soda
½ cup sugar
1 teaspoon salt
¾ cup water
½ cup grated coconut

Oil for deep frying

For garnish/topping
2 tablespoons toasted sesame seeds, for garnish

Coconut (or flavor of choice) ice cream, optional

Directions

1. In a bowl, sift the rice flour, baking soda, sugar, and salt together.
2. Add the water gradually while whisking, until there are no more lumps.
3. Stir in the grated coconut and mix to distribute evenly.
4. Heat the oil to 350°F in a deep pan, wok, or fryer.
5. Coat the banana slices with batter and fry, flipping over a few times, until golden brown.
6. Drain on paper towels, and sprinkle with toasted sesame seeds.
7. Serve with scoops of coconut ice cream (optional).

Conclusion

The recipes in this cookbook are a cultural journey into Thai influence on America's restaurant and food culture. Thai flavors and combination of spices are an exhilarating experience. I hope you have found your favorite Thai takeout dishes here, and that you will enjoy the experience of cooking it in your own home and giving it your own special touch. There is still so much joy to be found in preparing home-cooked dishes for loved ones or even for yourself.

Enjoy your cooking!

Cooking Conversion Charts

1. Measuring Equivalent Chart

Type	Imperial	Imperial	Metric
Weight	1 dry ounce		28g
	1 pound	16 dry ounces	0.45 kg
Volume	1 teaspoon		5 ml
	1 dessert spoon	2 teaspoons	10 ml
	1 tablespoon	3 teaspoons	15 ml
	1 Australian tablespoon	4 teaspoons	20 ml
	1 fluid ounce	2 tablespoons	30 ml
	1 cup	16 tablespoons	240 ml
	1 cup	8 fluid ounces	240 ml
	1 pint	2 cups	470 ml
	1 quart	2 pints	0.95 l
	1 gallon	4 quarts	3.8 l
Length	1 inch		2.54 cm

* Numbers are rounded to the closest equivalent

2. Oven Temperature Equivalent Chart

Fahrenheit (°F)	Celsius (°C)	Gas Mark
220	100	
225	110	1/4
250	120	1/2
275	140	1
300	150	2
325	160	3
350	180	4
375	190	5
400	200	6
425	220	7
450	230	8
475	250	9
500	260	

* Celsius (°C) = T (°F)-32] * 5/9

** Fahrenheit (°F) = T (°C) * 9/5 + 32

*** Numbers are rounded to the closest equivalent